Oliphant Margaret

Dies Irae

The Story of a Spirit in Prison

Oliphant Margaret

Dies Irae
The Story of a Spirit in Prison

ISBN/EAN: 9783744759618

Printed in Europe, USA, Canada, Australia, Japan

Cover: Foto ©ninafisch / pixelio.de

More available books at **www.hansebooks.com**

"DIES IRÆ"

" He that works me good with unmoved face,
  Does it but half; he chills me while he aids,—
  My benefactor, not my Brother-man."

—COLERIDGE.

"DIES IRÆ"

THE STORY OF A SPIRIT IN PRISON

WILLIAM BLACKWOOD AND SONS
EDINBURGH AND LONDON
MDCCCXCV

"DIES IRÆ."

PART I.

I HAD been very ill. I knew that. Strange whisperings had from time to time penetrated to my brain that were not intended for me to hear, and I knew from them that those in waiting upon me had given up all hope of my recovery.

At first I had rebelled, bitterly, clamorously. Still, as I appeared to lie, speechless, helpless, life was at fever-

A

heat in my brain, and my soul was rising up in fierce rebellion. In the full tide of youth and health to be singled out from the multitude to . . . die! There was surely injustice, cruel injustice, in it. "Threescore and ten years," I quoted, and I had but lived twenty-five. Never yet had I been denied anything that life could give, and now the common blessing of life itself was to be taken from me at a stroke.

I knew, I did not deny that I knew, that Death had never been a respecter of ages; but "All men think all men mortal but themselves": and that it should be I against whom the decree had gone forth—it was incredible.

That phase had passed; my fruitless wrath had spent itself; a few salt tears had gathered, and lain in the hollow cups of my eyes, and those that watched had looked more sadly than before upon me.

"Hush! she is dying!" I heard them say, as the first cock crew.

So the "Supreme Moment" was at hand; and, strangely enough, I was now beyond caring for it. Probably I was too weak to care.

"It must be very near," I thought, as I saw my good pastor kneel by my bedside, a look of intense earnestness contracting his features.

"She must not die. She shall not die. There is much for her to do on earth yet."

What did he mean? Was it work that I had left undone, and was he going to wrestle for my soul from out the very grip of death, as had done Luther, centuries ago, for his friend?

Ah! I was weary . . . too weary to think more. Through dimming sight I could just see the hospital nurse, a kindly dark-eyed woman, who seemed all eyes and cap and spotless linen, move round me as in a dream. Was she praying now too? And my cousin, whom they had brought four hundred miles, because I had no nearer relative, was she too sinking on her knees? . . . I was growing faint . . . fainter . . . the air was stifling! . . . I was struggling . . . panting . . . striving . . . Free! . . . drawing, it seemed to me, a long, long breath.

Where was I ?

Half-way through the room, half-way to the roof, turning with amazed eyes to look on the scene upon which I had just closed my eyes.

There was the kneeling pastor, with folded upraised hands and supplicating speech ; there the nurse, with bent head but professional watchfulness ; my little fair-haired cousin, her head buried on her hands ; strangest of all, there lay a figure outstretched under a snowy counterpane, that it was impossible to help recognising as myself. For one moment I saw distinctly the white, drawn face, sharpening in the death-agony, the closed eyes, the cup-like hollows filled with the cruel tears I had shed, the white hand on the counter-

pane. . . . A moment and all was dark.
I knew no more.

.   .   .   .   .   .

Had I been asleep, or was I awake
now ?

I was in the open air, a great sense of
space, of breath, of life about me.

Behind me lay a valley stretching into the dim distance, encompassed with
white mist. Shadows of human beings
were faintly discernible in its midst,
moving to and fro, and a very distant
hum of voices penetrated the air.   Here
and there I could see figures emerging
from its white cloud; sometimes in little
bands of three and four — sometimes
alone. Was that the earth that lay so
close to an encircling world ? . . .

Yes, and it lay behind me now.

What was beyond? I looked up with eager inquiry.

Before me rose in a long incline the green slope of a hillside that, through shaded ways, led to a level overshadowed by an amphitheatre of hills—hills whose peaks rose like great white crystals, roseate, golden-tipped, losing themselves in colour.

With bated breath and a strange thrill of expectancy, I asked myself, if perchance my feet had wandered to the threshold of Paradise; if these golden heights were where saints and angels congregated — where they "summered high in bliss upon the hills of God."

Nor did I fear that I had been deceived, when down the turf-clad path there moved towards me one, half-goddess, half-woman.

Where had I seen or heard of beauty such as hers before? Surely in some dream. Ah! I knew. . . . How often had I repeated with untiring delight—

> " Her robe, ungirt from clasp to hem
>   No wrought flowers did adorn ; . . .
> Her hair, that lay along her back,
>   Was yellow, like ripe corn."

There, in all the glory of the poet's picturing, she stood: a Blessed Damozel; and her soft slow steps were surely bringing her to me.

She was close to me. I was looking up into the blue depths of her eyes.

Yes:

> " They were deeper than the depths
>   Of water stilled at even."

But they were filled with a soft sadness that brought a shapeless fear to mingle with my wonder.

Was she sad for me, this Blessed Damozel? Her whole mien was one of gracious pity. . . . Was it for me? . . .

A faint feeling began to gather at my heart. The " hills of God " seemed very far away.

PART II.

WE were slowly climbing the steep, the Blessed Damozel and I. Her hand clasped mine in familiar touch. Her words of welcome had been sweet to my soul, for in saying them, through the depth of sorrow in her eyes there had shone the purest light of love.

"You . . . love me!" I had said, surprised into speech.

"I have loved you," she had murmured, "all your life upon the earth."

"Then I will fear no evil," I had answered, reassured, and clung to her outstretched hand.

As we went I pointed to the crystal heights on which the glory lay.

"I know them. I have read of them. They are the 'hills of God.' Are we going there?"

She lifted a reverent gaze to the far-off peaks.

"These are the 'hills of Holiness,'" she answered, and with averted gaze pursued her way.

The old faint fear crept coldly round my heart, and my gaze went fearfully forward. Visions of Paradise were slowly melting away from me. In their place the *Dies Iræ* began to repeat itself in my brain.

That Day of Wrath! that dreadful day! . . .

What was before me? . . . What awaited me? . . .

Half-way up the slope a murmur behind made me turn curiously. A little company was just emerging from the mist-filled valley, and following in our steps. My guide looked behind.

"Shall we wait for them?" she asked, and drew me aside into the shade of a grove of trees.

Before long they were nearing us. A little woman led by the hand by a fair guide somewhat like my own, but of a very different type of beauty. The flowing hair was dark, the figure fuller, and there was a very marked difference in her expression. It was of one that triumphed, and in her large dark eyes a light of victory shone. A little company followed them. A widow with streaming eyes, leading by the hand a boy and girl; a maiden, pale-faced and worn; a hard-featured woman, speaking volubly to a deaf audience, but with tears in her eyes.

"Who is she?" I asked, my gaze going back to the small central figure.

"A little maiden lady of seventy years, who left the world this morning. No, she does not look her years. It is the 'youth of the soul' that is on her face—immortal youth."

"And those who are with her, are they all dead? They somehow look different."

" No; these are the forms of those

who have loved her, and whose souls are longing after her so powerfully, that, unknown to themselves, they are here with her, testifying unconsciously to her love and sweet charity while among them."

"Did . . . did no one come with me?" I asked, shamed, I knew not why, before the question was well framed.

"She had seventy years of life, you only twenty-five," my friend answered, very sorrowfully. Her love would evidently fain cover a multitude of sins.

At this moment the group stopped almost opposite to us. The little face had the beauty of a child rather than that of an old woman.

"*She* has possessed her soul in innocency," I said, involuntarily. "But what does it all mean? I suppose she was kind to those people, but . . ."

"Keep your gaze fixed steadily upon her, and you will one by one see the different scenes of her life stand out in clear relief. I see them now, and as she moves up to higher planes, they will stand out in bolder and still bolder relief to every eye."

I steadied my gaze, and this is what I saw :—

I saw her as a girl seated at a piano, painfully imparting the most elementary knowledge of its use to a perplexed girl as old as herself.

"The girl has to win her bread by teaching. She is trying to fit her for

the battle. She has no money. She
is giving time . . . and love."

The scene had melted away.

Round her was a little house of mean
appearance. She was "on household
cares intent." A fretful woman was
extended on a sofa, speaking in querulous tones.

I looked to my guide.

"The sick woman is a worn-out
music-teacher, homeless, sick. She is
no relative, not even a friend, has but
the claim of weakness and want. The
little maiden lady had very small means.
She argued with herself that the only
way by which she could help her was
to do without any service herself, and
to use the cost of service in housing
and clothing this poor woman. Like

Dr Johnson's dependants, the music-mistress too often used her opportunities to grumble at her benefactress. But she is worshipping her to-day."

The woman of voluble speech was indeed on her knees before the little lady. I could hear her murmured thanks, and the troubled protest in response.

When I looked again, she was in other surroundings. The young widow and the boy and girl, whose figures were now fading into the mist, were clustered round her, younger and poorer.

"When the querulous old music-mistress died," spoke my guide, "the little lady vowed that she would still share her home with the homeless. Out of the crowd came this young widow, penniless, with a boy and girl to rear. These are the mourners whose true sorrow follows her. The widow's gratitude was not confined to words. Look at the home she made for her."

I saw a bright and happy household, holding the head in loving reverence, and she growing old among them.

"Now," said my guide, bringing me back to the present, "she will have her reward."

At this moment her guide stopped, her face wreathed with smiles, took a crown she had been carefully carrying, and stooping over her with infinite tenderness, placed it on her brows.

She turned her face towards me, alight with soft surprise, and I saw plainly written in letters of gold:—

"I was a stranger, and ye took me in."

Then they passed away, to where sweet strains of music called. We were alone, I with the tears gathered thick in my eyes.

"And I," looking round in bewilderment — "I have loved none, helped none, except through others; denied myself for none. What of me? . . . Ah! God will for Christ's sake forgive me. I died trusting in Him."

"God will for Christ's sake forgive you," said my sweet Damozel, solemnly, "but . . ."

"But what? Sweet Damozel, answer
me," for my guide was pursuing her
way with sorrowful mien.

"Yet one thing thou lackest," . . .
she quoted.

"'One thing thou lackest,'" I repeated after her. "'Sell all that thou
hast, and give to the poor.' But that,
. . . we were told that was not meant
literally."

"Its 'spirit' giveth life."

"Its 'Spirit'!" . . .

"Its spirit is Love, and Love is Ever-
lasting Life."

I was deeply bewildered.

"But"—a strange fear beginning to
gather round my heart—"the pains of
hell, they at least were an invention of
narrow-minded men, of whom Calvin

was the chief: not even for the wicked
do they exist!"

"I can believe in no hell," I went
on passionately, finding my guide slow
to answer, "for with it there could be
no heaven. I for one," daringly, being
deeply imbued with the latest sentiments I had listened to on earth—"I
could not be happy in the highest
heaven if I knew there was one poor
soul imprisoned in a hell."

I thought for a moment that my
Blessed Damozel was breathing a prayer
for me, so sad was the expression of her
uplifted eyes, and slowly but surely the
terrors of the Unknown began to en-
compass me about.

The air was growing colder, purer,
more difficult of breath, and an exces-

sive light was blinding me. We had reached the level.

It was, as I had seen from afar, an amphitheatre encircled by high hills; at first it seemed to be closed in entirely, but on looking closer and with straining gaze, I saw openings to right and to left.

With a flash of memory, words that had been familiar to me from childhood repeated themselves in my brain.

"And He set the sheep on His right hand, and the goats on His left."

"Where . . . do they lead?" I asked, with a strange sinking of the heart.

"To God," answered my guide, solemnly.

Oh, Day of Wrath! . . . Oh, Dreadful Day! . . . rhymed on in my brain.

"Come!" said my guide; and, with a terror growing ever greater at my heart, I followed to where, as I gazed on the two parting roads, there, out of the light a shape slowly formed itself, terrible in its beauty to any erring child of earth, for its beauty was the beauty of Holiness.

I fell prostrate at its feet. I closed my eyes in the dust. All my complacency fell from me as a garment; all the fair colouring with which I had clothed myself in imagination, melted like a breath before that pure presence. Petty self-deceivings, multiplied self-excusings, they were as if they had never been.

I had but one cry :—

"*God have mercy upon me, . . . Christ have mercy upon me.*"

Through the silence, and as if it were afar off, I heard the voice of my Blessed Damozel pleading for me.

"Lord, have pity upon her. She has sinned in ignorance."

. . . "*God have mercy upon me.*"

"She is yet of tender years. Only a third of the days allotted to man upon the earth have been granted to her."

. . . "*Christ have mercy upon me.*"

Strangely enough, although I lay prostrate as before, I could as plainly see my pleader and my Judge as if I had been standing upright before them ; and although I did not once

open my lips, a voice that yet seemed
mine took up speech against me,
almost without my will.

"*Mea culpa! mea culpa!*" . . .

"She brings none with her, it is true,
but she lived in a charmed circle.
Great wealth of this world's goods
were bequeathed to her. She has
known no poverty."

. . . "*God have mercy upon me.*"

"She has known no sorrow."

. . . "*Christ have mercy upon me.*"

"And," she went on, with pleading
earnestness, "she has known no love."

Then I knew, from the light on my
sweet guide's face, that this last plea
had somehow brought amelioration of
my sentence.

"Come!" she whispered low, and

I kissed the hem of her garment as she gently raised me.

"Where . . . are you leading me?" I asked in a new humility, when we had gone some distance. "But I know," . . . for she was slow to answer. "To Outer Darkness."

She stopped short, and wound her arms round my neck.

"It is indeed Outer Darkness," she answered, and made my spirit to fail with her word. "But, my love, you go on a quest that will end in victory, . . . on a high and holy quest."

"What quest?" raising weary eyes.

"The quest after Love."

"Ah! you said I had never known that. I thought I had."

"It is one thing to love, another

to be loved. On earth we too often crave for the second, and so miss the first. Yet the first is of God; the second of self."

"And when I find Love, shall I be safe?" sorrowfully enough.

Her eyes were very sad. "When you have ceased to ask after safety, you may come within reach of Love."

"Alas! you talk in riddles."

"Till the riddle is solved, you will not see God, for . . . 'God is Love.'"

I was sorely bewildered, and grievously faint at heart.

"Wherever I go, will you go with me?" I asked, clinging to her in a loneliness that was growing and growing in me.

"You will come back to me," she

answered, her eyes filling slowly with tears as she bent over me. "From the day that you were born, I have had you in my care. Now I may keep you but a very little longer. Ah! I am sad exceedingly for you, for I too have trodden every step of the way. I, like you, came hither trusting in the Christ, but with the very first lessons of the 'Religion of Love' unlearned; and only when you have conquered, shall I be free to live the wider life that lies beyond."

"There is a wider life beyond?"

"Yes!" the joy of all the ages future shining in her eyes, till she was transfigured to a beauty that thrilled me through and through, "a wider life beyond and beyond, and for ever beyond. We shall share it together."

" I shall never be like you ! " I cried, in despair.

" My love, you will one day awake in His likeness, . . . so shall I, . . . and we shall be satisfied."

But now and for me that Outer Darkness beckoned. Already I imagined that shadows were falling around us.

She read my thought.

" I shall wait for you at Dawn," she whispered.

" Have I then only one long night of horror and of pain before me ? " I asked, with conscious relief.

" We count no time here. A night is as a thousand years ; a thousand years as a night."

" You mean that Life is so intense, time is lost sight of."

" Yes."

" Why have you changed the word in the passage ? why night instead of day ? "

" There is no day where you go," she answered. " It is always night there."

I began to tremble exceedingly.

" But you will watch for me at Dawn ? " in accents that were now piteous entreaty. " You will not fail me ? "

" I shall watch with open arms for you at Dawn," she answered, and there-with fell on my neck and kissed me, mingling her tears with mine.

I thought I heard a sob, but it might have been my own sobbing breath, for my fears had overcome me, and I lay like a child in her arms, holding her fast.

As in a dream I felt the arms loosening slowly from round me, and then my own tenderly unclasped. I seemed to cling with all my might.

"Oh, Blessed Damozel!" I cried, "have pity! . . . Stay!" . . .

But it was of no avail. She was gone. I was alone, and swooning for fear and grief.

PART III.

WHEN I awoke, the shadows of
night were indeed around me.
Straining my gaze into their depths, I
could distinguish blacker shadows of
massive buildings rising higher and
higher on every hand; buildings on
buildings, dark, gloomy, with endless
passages winding in and out among
them—passages narrow, foul, and overshadowed with such darkness as lay on
my very soul; for surely it was not the
darkness of Nature alone that brooded
over that ghostly city.

From a height I looked down on it with ever-quickening gaze. Could these be human beings that crowded storey after storey of the towering masses of stone, and swarmed in swaying multitudes in every darkened passage? They did indeed seem to take shape to my curious gaze. Figures of old and young, sickly infants, and tottering old women, men and women of all ages, mixed in a motley crowd; and ever and anon, to my shrinking ear, from the whole came up a confused wailing of many voices, sounding, it seemed to me, every note of pain, from the feeble wail of infancy to that of torture unendurable, while loud-mouthed curses, that made my very flesh creep for fear, mingled from time to time with the sounds.

c

It is, I think, Jean Paul Richter who has recorded his belief that of all Hells the Hell of sound is the worst; and I knew then, as I had never known before, what he meant. It was no long time till, after listening to cry after cry, I put my hands to my ears in the vain endeavour to escape from it all. But no device of earth availed here. There was no closing of the ears. The increasing wail waxed ever louder and more bitter; I even grew to distinguish a horrible laughter mingling itself with it, till, when at last a terror-filled shriek rang and rang through the darkened air, I could bear it no longer. I threw myself on my knees and added my cry to theirs.

"God in Heaven, what have they

done, to be so tormented?" I cried. "Is there no mercy in heaven or earth to help them?"

A voice, stern, resolute, sounded in my ear. It bade me rise; and looking up, I found by my side one of terrible aspect, awful in a majesty that made me cower before him.

"Who art thou?" I did not dare to ask, but he had read and answered my thought.

"I am the Avenging Angel," he answered.

"To these poor people," I said, with an indignant thrill.

"Of these poor people," he answered. And although I knew not what he meant, I shrank before him.

"You are . . . their . . ."

But even as I spoke, another of those terror-laden shrieks rent the air and startled me out of all self-control.

"What does it mean?" I sobbed, in almost equal terror.

"It means that cruelty is rampant, and there is none to check it; that lust is unbridled, and the innocent flee before it; that avarice stalks unheeded throughout the land, leaving famine and desolation behind. Look and learn."

They were words my Blessed Damozel had used; but they were repeated now with a sternness of tone that made me tremble as before a judge. No compassion shone in the eyes of the Avenging Angel as he bent them on me.

I turned my gaze where he directed, and found that by some strange means he had contrived to throw a strong light down on a pair of figures in the far depth of the valley—a pair clasped in each other's arms; a husband and wife. The woman was wan and worn to a shadow; the man scarcely better.

"Avarice has been on their track for years," said my guide. "She is slowly dying, but she has possessed her soul in patience. She will be at rest to-night."

"But why are they here at all? What sin did they commit?"

There was no answer. The thoughts of the Avenging Angel were far from me.

"To-morrow at dawn I shall set her

free, and she shall sleep till then. But
. . . 'woe to him by whom the offence
cometh.'"

Why should all the graciousness pass
from his face when he turned to me?
Why should I have to shrink again
into the attitude of a culprit? I did
not dare to ask the question I was
longing to have answered. Did death
reign here as in the world? for no
such possibility had entered my imagination. But questioning was lost
sight of in a new terror.

A cry as of a hunted animal rent the
air and startled me into a new agony
of fear.

"What? . . . what is that?"

For answer the strange light fell with
lurid gleam on a fleeing maiden of tender

years and a monster in human shape pursuing.

My heart stood still, then leapt with sudden horror.

"O God, he gains on her! . . . Stop him! . . . You are an angel! Oh . . ."

My shrieks were mingling with the maiden's as I fell on my face to shut out the hideous horror.

It was long before I raised streaming eyes to my companion.

"You could have helped, you would not move."

"I am her Avenger," he answered, grimly.

"You will hurl her destroyer to the lowest hell," I said.

"Nay, not him alone."

"On whom will vengeance fall?" I asked, eagerly.

"These are the hidden things of God," he answered, solemnly. "Each goeth to his own place."

Each to his own place, and I was here. What had such scenes as those I was witnessing to do with me? . . .

Even as we spoke a great hum of angry voices was coming again within hearing, swelling as it rose and rose, ever nearer, and bringing with it a new horror before which my spirit quailed. Was there to be no rest for me through all this weary night? I shrank before the ever-growing tumult : children crying, women shrilly calling, men cursing.

"Oh, I cannot bear more! . . . The

night is hideous with sound. A moment, I pray you, of rest. Shut out the sounds from my ears but for one brief moment. Let me dream, were it only for a moment, that I am again back in my old home, all barbarous sounds shut out. . . . I am a weak and tenderly reared girl. . . . Such sights and sounds as I have seen and heard to-night, I have never even dreamt of. What, . . . what is happening now? . . . Ah, spare me! No more light, I pray. But, my God, what is that? . . ."

"Cruelty rampant: the victims are at its mercy."

"Is there none to help? none to answer to such cries?"

"The few help; the many disregard.

But the Lord will avenge," solemnly, "and I am His servant."

He was awful as he spoke, for the valley rang with execrations, strange oaths, piteous weeping.

I went back to my pleading.

"A moment of respite, I pray you, . . . I am sick at heart." . . .

What was happening? A strange light was spreading far and wide in a large semicircle, leaving the valley below in deeper gloom than before. The night was become light about us. I gazed as one in a dream at fair gardens stretching down gentle slopes, at stately mansions, at delicate women and strong-limbed men, strolling through softly carpeted rooms or lounging on low settees. Children like to little angels played merrily, and soft laughter welled out to us.

As I looked, recognition slowly came to me. I had got my prayer.

"It is what I left behind!" I cried, in rapture. "Ah, how good it was!"

For a brief moment I gazed, forgetting all the horrors I had gone through. Alas! it was only for a moment. My guide touched me on the shoulder.

"How good it was!" I repeated, ere I responded.

His face was sterner than before as he looked down on me. Slowly raising his hand with an ominous gesture, he pointed to the deep Valley of Shadow I had for the moment been allowed to forget.

"And what of them?" he asked.

I followed his gaze. I was growing truly bewildered.

"What! . . . Do they lie so near?"

"So near that although those in the Valley cannot climb to those who 'dwell at ease,' yet those dwellers at ease can go to the weary and tormented and save them if they will."

"If they will!" I cried, indignantly. "Who would rest if they could help that struggling multitude?" . . .

. . . A curious thing was happening. Slowly the mists enshrouding the Valley were rolling away before my eyes, and as they lifted themselves, the place was assuming a strangely familiar shape. Were not these the towers and fastnesses of my own town rising out of the crowd? Was that streak of grey not the river with its bridges, that separated the old town from the new? Could it be? Was that Valley of wicked strife and dire poverty and cruel disease indeed the picturesque valley in the midst of my childhood's home? Was this the Valley of Shadow unspeakable I had been contemplating?

It was night. The gas-lit streets were swarming with a swaying multitude, the crowded houses still poured forth their inmates. . . . They were recognisable for such men and women and children as I had grown up among. At this moment the old town clock I had known from a child tolled out the hour. I counted the strokes mechanically.

"Twelve o'clock! . . . Midnight!"
I said, without thinking.

"Midnight!" repeated my guide, as
the last stroke died away. "It is now
the 'Day of Rest.'"

Oh! hideous mockery.

"And that is . . ."

"The town where you and they were
born."

"And these are . . ."

"Your sisters . . . and brothers."

"It has been a morbid dream," I
cried. "I have had a nightmare."

But almost before I had dared to
uplift my voice, the mists fell as before
on all around. I was standing alone
with my guide on the mountain-side.
Below us stretched the darkened Valley
like a Lake of Gloom in the heart of

the pretty town : worse than all, that wail of all the weary, that cry of all the suffering, was filling again the void.

"Where are the watchmen?" I asked, with a tone of earth in my voice, which my guide must have recognised.

"In the fray," answered my guide, "adding to it, saving some, too late for others. They perhaps are least likely to think your dream morbid."

And, indeed, with that weary, weary wail in my ears, it was difficult to repeat my words.

"My God, it is too awful!" I cried in despair, for sight was now being added to sound; and when I would fain have closed both eyes and ears, it was to find as before that no such escape was possible. "It is too awful! It is hell indeed!"

And so saying, I sank to earth.

"No happiness was possible for you in Heaven, while one poor spirit lay in Hell," gibed a mocking voice in my ear.

Without looking up, I knew that my stern guide was gone, and that his place had been taken by an imp of darkness, who was grinning at my discomfiture.

"Beautiful dreamer of fair sentiments!" reviled another voice. "Imaginative sympathy is so fine a thing. And so easy." . . .

"Learn what this meaneth," spoke one solemnly in passing; "'I will have mercy, and not sacrifice.'" . . .

. . . "'And though I bestow all my goods to feed the poor, . . . and have not Love,'" quoted another sorrowfully, "'it profiteth me nothing.'" . . .

PART IV.

"ONE night is as a thousand years." . . .

I was in the arms of my Blessed Damozel, sobbing my heart out on her breast.

"At last. . . . At last the day had dawned and set me free, and, as I had never doubted she would be, there, waiting on the fair hillside, had stood my sweet and blessed Lady, the first rays of sunshine lying on her golden hair, her white arms outstretched, her eyes full of tenderest sympathy, and deep with unforgotten sorrow.

I could not speak. I could not bring before her mind one picture of the horrors I had undergone. I could only cling to her neck and sob, . . . and sob.

"I know it all," she whispered. "I too have gone every step of the way."

It seemed too cruel. She too, my Blessed Damozel.

"No! Not cruel, love." . . . Did ever saint or angel say that word as did my sweet lady? It fell as balm on the wounded spirit. "Not cruel. I . . . listen, love," . . . for indeed I was refusing to listen—"I would go through every pang of that time to gain what I have gained."

It was a spiritless questioning I undertook.

"What was your gain?"

"The Crown of Life: Love," she answered.

I had forgotten. It was a quest after Love I had been supposed to be sent forth on. I had not even once remembered it.

"I . . . have gained nothing," I answered.

"Ah, yes, you have." . . .

"What?"

"Knowledge." . . .

I was too weary for answer. I dropped my head upon her fair bosom. She understood, and presently we reclined on the slope together, I held fast in her arms, the soft air of summer wrapping us round, the trill of birds in our ear, the clear trickling of a brook close by. But what were they all to the loving embrace that held me: tender, true, for all the Eternity that lay before us?

We were " as the angels of God."

PART V.

" A THOUSAND years is as a
day."

It had seemed no more than a day,
a too short day, till again the shadows
were falling thick around me, and I
stood alone with reluctant feet at the
entrance to that world of darkness I
had learned to name hell.

A force it was useless to resist was
impelling me forward, and yet it was
only to be met by sounds and sights
that as strongly seemed to force me
back at every step. Ah, for a door

of escape! . . . And yet. . . . One glimmer of intelligence shone like a star in a dark firmament, where all was blackness before.

My Blessed Damozel had trodden every step of the way — nay, Christ Himself had trodden it. . . . I could never be as Christ, or even as my sweet lady, but there might be for me also sweet to be gained by the bitter.

I was moving ever down the slope, nearer and nearer to the black masses of people, deeper into the shadow of gloom, till I was at length myself one of the multitude that swayed this way and that, in the narrow alleys and in the open squares.

Caught into the stream, I had small

time given me to think. There at my feet was a little child, disfigured, marred in visage, probably all that was criminal in embryo, but still a child, weak, helpless; and a reeling madman, emerging from the darkness, had his foot raised to kick. With the old cry of pain, I sprang to interpose, but it was only to discover what I had for the moment forgotten, that I was not now of Earth. I could interpose no human body between; the child fell with a moan, and a passer-by lifted it, while another promptly implanted a blow on the drunken wretch, which he was too insensible to feel.

I turned and fled. The old horrors of my night were indeed begun. It was as if all the peaceful homes were hidden from my sight, and light, a strange lurid light, that of itself lent a horrible clearness to the pictures, was poured down on every revolting sight that a city at its lowest can show. Nothing that was not of Earth, and already familiar to me through the newspaper columns of the day; it was only that the light detached them from the whole, and for a time I was made to see them, and only them, in a succession of horrors that was agonising.

Yes, they were all familiar.

That, before which I shrieked, would to-morrow be reported as a murder "under peculiarly revolting circumstances;" that which made me sicken to the verge of unconsciousness would

be included in the annual statistics of
the Society for Prevention of Cruelty
to Children as one of the ten thousand
cases that had been brought under their
notice; and this, where I had stood at
the girl's elbow, and wept, and implored
her to turn from the temptation before
her, would be mentioned as a sad case
of suicide.

That fair young girl had moved me
greatly. A cloud rested on her brain.
Temporary illness had some months
before stopped the weekly wage for
which she worked, and, in her need,
she had fallen behind in her payments.
The burden of debt had ever since
pressed heavily upon her; in the en-
feebled state of her health, it had taken
undue hold of her imagination, till now,

with darkened vision, she stood like a creature at bay, on the brink of the Unknown.

"Help will come to-morrow," I had pleaded.

"There have been a great many to-morrows," had been her answer, "and no help came."

"They do not know," I pleaded, for the girl looked fiercely up at the gardened slopes where the helpers lay.

"They do not seek to know."

"Oh yes, they do. If I had known." . . .

"They know that we are here, and that we have not bread. They know that where there is not bread there is hunger, and sickness, and bitterness, and loss of self-restraint."

"They do not know that you have not bread."

But as I spoke, my confidence melted from me. I remembered that it was only the week before my illness, that I had sat at my comfortable drawing-room fire, brooding over the latest results of inquiries in East London. Twenty-five, if not thirty per cent, of the people living that day below the Poverty Line, one in four not knowing where 'Daily Bread' was to come from : one in every ten 'Very poor.' This very girl must have been one of these. I had had a week to do it in. Why had I not gone down on the spot into the dark gully, on whose banks we had builded our pleasant homes — why had I not gone down, and putting my arms round her, said to her, "Sister, you must know no more want, while I am here to share with you"?

O God, if I had but done it, if I could but do it now! No one could possibly object to charity like that; they could not say it was "demoralising." For that had been my great "problem" in these now far-off days. I laughed my problem to scorn as I stood close to my poor sister.

"Sweet, my love," I said to her, my whole heart going out in a strange yearning that it had never known before, "have patience but a little while. I know good women over there who would be shocked beyond measure if they thought you were on the point of taking away your own life, because

of hunger, and cold, and misery. Let
me but have time to go to them, and
awake them from their slumber, and
you will see what life can be yet."

She smiled bitterly at what she
thought was her own better nature
speaking.

"Ah, yes, I know well," she answered,
with impatience in her voice, and her
eye alight with a pained bewilderment,
"that if I could bring myself to be a
beggar and go from door to door, I
should gather half - crowns in plenty;
but 'to beg I am ashamed.' . . . Yet
bread I must have or I cannot live.
And my work does not suffice. My
flesh fails for very weariness before
I have coppers enough to buy more
food to give strength for more work.

Why should I go on? . . . I have none to care whether I live or die. . . . There is rest here!" . . . pointing to the flood below.

"Oh, it is awful!" I said. "So much given, and yet blood at our doors."

"It is not money we want," she answered, almost fiercely, her intellect waking up with sudden flash to its clearest. "Yes, indeed, showers of half-crowns are falling, and the scramble for them is not good to see. More and more joining the clamouring crowd." . . . She suddenly laughed a horrible laugh. "Four coffins finding their way to one man's deathbed, sent by four different societies!—one will be enough for me. . . . Ah! I am sick, sick,

weary of it all. The scramble for the
falling coins, the 'crumbs from the
rich man's table,' and those who have
no heart or too much pride for the
scramble . . . dying. Listen!" her
eye gleaming fire, as she laid her hand
on an imaginary listener—or was vision
lent to her, that she could see as well
as hear me?—"I tell you, tell you truly,
what we want is not money but . . .
Love. One loving woman to one
struggling sister; one loving brother to
one fallen comrade in the fight. One
and one alone: caring as a sister would
care, not once leaving her till she sees
all her wrongs righted, or till her weakness or poverty is a thing of the past.
Ah!" looking up to the gardened slopes,
passionate pity gathering in her eyes,

"were I ever to become rich, would it be possible for me, I wonder, to forget it all; to forget my toiling sisters, going wearily home after hours of sunshine spent in close rooms, home to bare meals, too tired to be amused, if there were amusement provided; only too thankful if kindly sleep await them, instead of perplexing care, care of how the week's debts are to be met? Would it be possible for me to forget, I wonder, that there must be many and many doing as I have so often done, toiling in spirit with the weary car - horses, feeling that life with them and with me was much the same: on and on: the whip of want, if one threatens to stop? Ah! if I were but one of these," again looking up to the gardens

E

above, tears in her voice and gathering
in her eyes, " I would take one at least
from this sorry den and make her life
so fair for her ; and she should know no
want any more, nor care any more,—
just as if I were her true sister,—nor
bitterness of dependence, for there is
no bitterness where Love is, nor shame
of beggary.   But . . . it is easy to
dream dreams.   If I were as they, I
should no doubt grow self - absorbed
and self-sufficient even as they.   Ah !
. . . what nonsense it all is !   Only,
if my dream came to pass, there could
be no talk then of 'over - lapping
Charity !' " and she laughed a laugh
that was not good to hear.   "Oh !"
raising her hands to her head, " I
shall be glad when my ears are deaf-

ened that I cannot hear; the mockery of it all is too great."

And once more there settled down upon her brain the cloud I now knew myself powerless to combat.

"Let me be your sister," I would fain have said; but I knew, before the words were spoken, that it was in vain. My punishment was, that I could not give her help. My love and longing had come all too late.

Yet I had deemed myself a follower of Him who said: "Love one another, as I have loved you."

I sought excuses. It was truly the sin of ignorance. My youth! . . . Had I then been so young? If one is not to rise to gracious womanhood in twenty-five years, when will the

awakening come? I had surely not
been too young to know what women
of my own age were suffering.

"How old are you?" I found myself
asking.

"Twenty-five. My birthday falls to-
morrow."

Twenty-five, and weary of life: weary
of disappointment rather; for of life,
bright, beautiful, young life, with its joy
in colour and movement, this sister of
mine had known nothing.

Just then one passed close by us, in
satin and pearls, with rouged cheek and
glittering white teeth, that laughed us
to scorn.

She was a NANA, let loose as a
scourge on the weaklings of the day,
scattering fortunes as a child scatters

bonbons, sending youths forth stripped penniless, as the fruit of a week's folly; but for herself, all the pleasures a life of sin could give were hers. My companion lifted her head at sound of the laughter, and shuddered as she passed. There was again a flash of sanity.

"I was once as beautiful as she."

"But you were not tempted. . . ."

"Never. This," pointing to the flowing tide, "is better than that."

I stooped to hide the blinding tears.

"Sister! . . ." I said, "I am not worthy. . . . Ah! . . ."

She had not heard me. Like a bird she had flashed through the gloom into the tide below, and the water had opened to receive her.

What angel would greet *her* as she

emerged from the mist? I thanked
heaven that she went into God's good
keeping, and, as the shrill laughter of the
woman of sin came again on the still
air, once more I thanked God for her.

Turning slowly back to the crowded
maze, with weeping eyes and humbled
heart, I was conscious of a curious
change in myself. What was it? The
lagging step was gone, the intense un-
willingness to move forward. The bitter
outcry that the burden laid upon me was
more than I could bear was no more.
In its place there had come a strong
impulse forward into the heart of the
crowd; a great longing to take some
one of them to me, the weaker the
better, and push the way for him or her
and myself out from the shadow into the

light. I had forgotten even my Blessed Damozel in the strong interest that had sprung up in my heart. . . . Yes! in my heart, . . . that was then the secret.

My heart was awake . . . at last! Awake in its own regal right, . . . asking nothing, . . . giving all. . . .

"And if I love thee, what is that to thee?" rang down a century's length and was understood.

And pity as an emotion was swallowed up in pity as a motive.

Instead of closing my ears to the continuous wail of pain, my eyes to the saddening sights, my arms seemed to stretch themselves out in pure yearning towards that sorrowing multitude, my feet were swift to take me into the heart of it.

One loving woman to one struggling sister! . . . that at least was within reach : to have her and hold her, and care for her and love her . . . for ever! That at least, . . . what more the future might unfold . . . I could leave.

Alas! I had forgotten, . . . I was not of earth, and could help have come from heaven, these poor souls had been helped long ere now. No such heaven opened before me as I had been picturing. It was to be my fate to wander sadly, helpless, prayerful, in ever-present pain of powerlessness, among that weary multitude—suffering with them, learning from them, feeling myself unworthy to tie the shoe-latchet of the least of them. It was they who were to save me, not I them.

PART VI.

THE sorrow was all gone from my sweet lady's eyes as they rested lovingly on mine. For the day had dawned once more, the shadows had melted away from about me, and I was standing in the early sunshine, my hands in hers, in a strong grasp of new strength and comradeship. Was I dreaming, or was that the same light of triumph on her countenance which had so impressed me in the dark-eyed saint who had led the little old lady of seventy to her Lord, and was she triumphing for me? . . .

But my heart was too full of enlarged
life to allow me to linger for more than
a moment on this new impression.   I
hastened to share it with her.

"Sweet sister, . . ." I did not notice
the new equality. . . . "I have found it.
I know . . . what it is to love."

The grasp on my hands grew tighter.

"And although there," glancing back,
"and for a little time, it is indeed sorrow, . . . for all eternity it will be joy."

Ah! the deep, deep joy that glowed
in the eyes of my listener!

"They are coming, are they not, . . .
one by one; all those who have one
spark of the Divine in them? And I
know now why you pleaded for me so
earnestly as my excuse that I had not
known   poverty,   for   indeed   'Hardly

shall they that have riches enter into the Kingdom.' It is poverty that has taught many of these poor souls that lesson of self-forgetfulness, which I altogether failed in learning. And sorrow is teaching others; and all, . . . all except that lowest grade of all, that one in every hundred, which none yet have had power to raise or help—all are living nearer to the lessons of life, than are many of the dwellers at ease on the hillside."

No word would she speak in answer, but her look was eloquent of triumph at every word I spoke, and pleaded for more, . . . more. . . .

"Yes, they are surely closer to each other in their struggling and striving, failing and winning, than are the rich

they envy. It is true, they stretch out
weary limbs at night, and aching frames
are laid on hard couches; but often and
often, even then, their hearts 'make holi-
day.' For often, too tired to sleep, they
allow their minds to dwell on the hard
task completed, the righteous debt paid,
want once more tided over for some one
dearer than self! Yes, through it all,
round the hearts of the loving among
them—and there are many such—there
never ceases to play that warmth of tender feeling, that only stern workers know
who toil for those they love. Ah! to
stand in the breach for the weak! . . .
above all, for the weak that we love! . . .
I have learned, sweet sister, from that
struggling multitude, that there is no joy
on earth to compare with that; there is,

there can be, no joy in earth or heaven greater than that." . . .

Upon which my Blessed Damozel loosened suddenly her grasp of my hands, put her arms round my neck, and our lips met in a kiss that was full of promise. It told that we were one in intent and purpose: that we loved one another, but we loved humanity more; and the joy of the future would be, that, hand in hand, we would go forth together, as "ministers of grace" to "do His pleasure."

"God bless all those who are trying to add to the sum of human happiness; God bless all those who are trying to lessen the sum of human pain," had prayed Sunday after Sunday the clergyman of our parish.

Ah! we should be henceforth among "the blessed of God."

When she drew it back, my Blessed Damozel's face shone with such beauty that I found myself saying in fresh wonderment, "How very beautiful you are!"

She smiled. "Come," she said.

And she led me to a lake clear as crystal.

"Look."

I bent and saw reflected in it two faces side by side. One was that of my companion, smiling back at me with a beauty that again filled me with a great sense of gladness. I loved beauty. I loved her beauty.

Then I turned to the other, and as I looked my wonder grew and grew; and as my wonder grew, the eyes in the looking-glass we had found grew larger and softer and softer, till they filled with tears.

"I . . . cannot be . . . like that." . . .

"You are like that," whispered my sister; "for that is 'the beauty of Holiness.'"

"But I am not holy!" said I, in still deeper amazement.

"Holiness is . . . an Infinite Sympathy for others," she whispered again. "You remember?" . . .

Yes, I remembered a sister on Earth had spoken that, and I had thought it very beautiful.

While I was still pondering I felt my companion turn from me, and wafted on the soft air, there came from the direction in which she turned a distant sound of rejoicing.

I raised my head and turned with her. "What . . . is it?" I asked.

"The 'Songs of them that triumph,'" said my Blessed Damozel, her eye lighting, her body swaying forward; 'the Shouts of them that feast.' Hark! they are calling to us, calling to you and to me. . . . Come."

.   .   .   .   .   .

With a long, long sigh I was awaking.

Awaking to what? To the twilight of a darkened chamber, to the far, far-off sound of familiar voices: now to the sight of a familiar face.

It was the hospital nurse. She took my hand.

I could hear her speak. I could catch what she was saying.

"She is conscious, I am sure. She pressed my hand."

Another far - off voice: our clergyman's. "It was prayer that brought her back. For a moment the soul seemed separate from the body, but I was intent she should not die; with her powers, her riches, her youth, she had so much to do in the world yet. . . . I *would* not let her go."

I struggled for utterance.

"So much to do in the world yet! One loving woman to one struggling sister, . . . to have her and hold her, . . . and care for her and love her,— above all, . . . to love her . . . for ever." . . .

"She is wandering again," said the nurse.

Was I wandering? Am I wandering still? . . . Has it been a dream, a dream and nothing more?

THE END.

PRINTED BY WILLIAM BLACKWOOD AND SONS.

" He that works me good with unmoved face,
    Does it but half; he chills me while he aids,—
    My benefactor, not my Brother-man."

                                    —COLERIDGE.